Life Lessons from the Jungle:

Naming the Elephant

The Art of Solving Problems and Making Decisions

by

BARBARA J. MCADOO

Note for Librarians: A cataloguing record for this book is available from Library and Archives Canada at www.collectionscanada.ca/amicus/index-e.html
ISBN 1-4120-6094-x

Printed on paper with minimum 30% recycled fibre. Trafford's print shop runs on "green energy" from solar, wind and other environmentally-friendly power sources.

TRAFFORD PUBLISHING™
Offices in Canada, USA, Ireland and UK
This book was published *on-demand* in cooperation with Trafford Publishing. On-demand publishing is a unique process and service of making a book available for retail sale to the public taking advantage of on-demand manufacturing and Internet marketing. On-demand publishing includes promotions, retail sales, manufacturing, order fulfilment, accounting and collecting royalties on behalf of the author.

Book sales for North America and international:
Trafford Publishing, 6E–2333 Government St.,
Victoria, BC V8T 4P4 CANADA
phone 250 383 6864 (toll-free 1 888 232 4444)
fax 250 383 6804; email to orders@trafford.com
Book sales in Europe:
Trafford Publishing (UK) Ltd., Enterprise House, Wistaston Road Business Centre,
Wistaston Road, Crewe, Cheshire CW2 7RP UNITED KINGDOM
phone 01270 251 396 (local rate 0845 230 9601)
facsimile 01270 254 983; orders.uk@trafford.com
Order online at:
trafford.com/05-0995

10 9 8 7 6 5 4 3 2 1

Dedicated to all who search,
for they will be rewarded with
knowledge—may it bring
them wisdom as well.

"The elephant is a very large animal," said the Rajah kindly. "Each man touched only one part. Perhaps if you put the parts together, you will see the truth. Now, let me finish my nap in peace."

"He is right," said the first blind man. "To learn the truth, we must put all the parts together. Let's discuss this on the journey home."

From *The Blind*
Men and the Elephant
An old Hindu tale

PREFACE

In an era when whimsy is often disparaged, this book, *Naming the Elephant,* uses an unconventional approach to discuss an integral function of everyday life: solving problems and making decisions.

Naming the Elephant is an amusing tale, in which co-workers sent to a seminar suddenly find themselves in an unexpected setting. With a set of rules entirely different from those in their day-to-day lives, they quickly discover they are expected to complete a simple task that can only be accomplished by pooling talents and sharing experiences.

The interesting personalities of the participants, along with the circumstances in which they find themselves, create an entertaining backdrop against which important lessons are taught — and learned.

Follow Loki, Leo, Petra, and the others as they learn truths about themselves, and those with whom they associate on a daily basis, while helping one another in *Naming the Elephant*.

ACKNOWLEDGEMENTS

I owe a huge debt of gratitude to many people, but most especially to my husband, David Kenny, whose love, encouragement, and support made the creation of this book possible in the first place!

To all my "editors," thanks so very much:

- Barbara Hunter, for your patient reading, rereading, and correcting...especially the commas!
- Mary Anne Costello, for your suggestions...all of them.
- Janet Hobson, for your enthusiasm and ideas.
- Jackie Brannon, for agreeing to review and comment.
- Katie (K-D) Jarvis for taking the time while on vacation to read *Elephant*, and for your enthusiastic evaluation.

I truly appreciate your taking time from your own lives to do this for me!

And, to the men and women of Sonitrol...thanks for the inspiration!

NOTE: This book, as with any piece I've ever written, has become like a child to me. After a while, it becomes difficult, if not impossible, to see the flaws...any there are belong completely to me and not to those who've helped with its editing.

CONTENTS

CHAPTER 1

A DIFFERENT KIND OF SEMINAR

"Look at this sign! Can you believe it?" grumbled Lon, a tall and somewhat disheveled man with arms and legs that seemed too long for his body.

The sign read:

Life-Changing Seminar
Today Only!
Please—
Leave Closed Minds at the Door!

"Well," continued Lon, "I guess this is the place. The boss told us to be here, so, here's where we have to waste an entire day listening to some know-it-all tell us what we're doing wrong in our lives."

Looking at him from the corner of her eye, Petra, a short, energetic woman with bright red hair and brilliant green eyes, grimaced. "Did you happen to notice the sign says to leave closed minds at the door? Could you, for once, approach something from a perspective other than negative? Man, I've had enough of your negativity. Find someone else to hang with today. I'll see you at the office tomorrow! I, for one, plan to enjoy this meeting!"

With that, Petra strode into the meeting room off the opulent hotel lobby, eager to begin the day. Scratching his head, Lon watched her leave.

"Women," Lon mumbled. "Go figure. Well, guess I'll just find myself a seat in the back of the room, maybe get some shuteye…won't be a total waste of my time that way."

As Lon entered the room, he noticed something strange. Instead of the cool air conditioning to which he was accustomed, the air seemed very humid. Lush, green foliage grew in abundance, with large trees and other vegetation. Lon listened in astonishment to chirping, grunting, and screeching sounds. A sudden roar made him jump in alarm. Startled, he whirled about. Lon could no longer see the entrance to the room.

Where the door should have been became a jungle path. Ahead, the path opened to a gathering place that was filled…with…animals!

"Ah, Loki, you've finally decided to join us. Come, sit by me," said a deep Voice.

"It's Lon, and who are you? And where are you?" asked Lon. "And what happened to the seminar…and what are all these animals doing here?"

"So many questions, Loki," replied the Voice. "I hope you'll be able to answer them all very soon."

"Why do you call me Loki? My name is Lon, not Loki!" Lon exclaimed, stomping his feet in frustration.

"Why, because of your personality, naturally," responded the Voice. "Are you not aware of Loki from Norse mythology, who always got into trouble, then managed to worm his way out by wit and trickery? Look into yourself and you will find Loki, so Loki is what I shall call you."

The other animals laughed. "He's got you pegged," said Parrot.

"Oh be quiet, Petra," responded Loki. "Hey! Petra, why is your voice coming out of that parrot's mouth? Is this some sort of joke? Oh, I know, this is some deal with ventriloquism, isn't it?" As the Voice chuckled, and the circle of animals joined the laughter, Loki became irritated and stomped his feet and yelled.

"Oh, stop it, Lon, I mean Loki!" exclaimed Petra Parrot. "Your monkey screams hurt everyone's ears!"

"Monkey screams," yelled Loki. "I'm a man, not a monkey!"

"Oh yeah," drawled a voice from behind him. "Better take a look at yourself. You certainly look like a monkey to me."

"Yeah, well, what do you know, Leo?" replied Loki contemptuously. "You may be the big cheese in the office, but you sure ain't no king of beasts." Hearing a growl, Loki looked around. Spying the lion, he backed up and said, "Whoa, big fella, sorry I didn't see you!"

"Oh, Loki, it's me…Leo," answered Leo Lion. "Look around you; we're all animals now, animals that represent our personalities. I am, indeed, the lion! And you, you are a very silly monkey!" Smiling a toothy lion smile, and giving a loud roar, Leo padded toward Loki, demonstrating his authority.

Screaming in fear, Loki swung up into the branches of the nearest tree. "Leave me alone you big bully!"

"Thank you, Leo," said the Voice. "That's enough for now. I believe you have convinced Loki of his role here. Leo is correct, Loki. You've all become the animals your personalities represent. The persona is accurate, and each of you must resolve how your personality has determined the particular animal shape. We are not here today, though, to examine your personality, but to answer a simple question."

"Oh, man," moaned Loki Monkey. "Just when I thought my day couldn't get any worse, now we gotta answer some dumb question."

"Quiet!" roared the lion.

"Oh, sorry Lion, I mean Leo, I mean..." stumbled Loki. "I, um, was just sayin' how, um, er, how we gotta get serious about the seminar, and er..."

"Ah, ha," interjected Petra, laughing. "Yep, he's Loki, all right!"

The rest of the animals joined in the laughter. Loki angrily shook the branch on which he was standing and was startled when a voice quite near him said, "S-s-s-stop that wiggling or I'll give you s-s-s-such a bite."

Looking about, Loki saw a small green snake very close to his face. "Oh, oh, sorry Snake," Loki replied nervously. "Er, is that you, Sam? How'd you get to be a Snake, anyway?"

"Yes-s-s-s, it's-s-s-s me, S-s-s-sam, the S-s-s-snake. And if you have to as-s-s-k me that ques-s-s-stion, you don't really know me." With that, Sam slithered up the tree trunk and into the foliage above.

"Oh, okay, um, see you later, Sam," replied Loki, and under his breath, continued, "and maybe not!"

"All right, everyone," announced the Voice. "Let's begin."

"Come on, show yourself." This interjection came, of course, from Loki. At some movement in the jungle just beyond the circle, he continued, "Are you shy or something…all I can see is what looks like, well, it looks kinda like a gray wall. Are you hiding behind that wall?" He swung easily from his perch to another in a tree closer to the edge of the clearing. "Hey, now I can see a part of you, I think. I see a long tube, or pipe, or somethin'. Are you attached to some sort of life support system? Are you some kind of alien?"

"Wait," piped a small voice, "I know what he looks like, or at least how big he is…I saw a huge column! He must be a giant to sit on a chair with a leg that big!"

"No," answered the Voice with a chuckle. "I'm not shy, and I'm certainly not an alien, nor all that gigantic, at least in comparison to many things in this world. Be patient and you'll see me in good time." The Voice continued, "For now, pay attention, for I have much to tell in our time together. The nature of our seminar is a discussion of the steps to solving problems and making decisions. We make decisions all the time, good ones and bad ones, and sometimes we decide not to decide."

"You said steps to making decisions," interjected Petra. "What kind of steps?"

"Yeah," added Loki. "I don't recall ever taking any steps when I decide what I'm gonna eat for lunch."

"Ha!" laughed Leo. "That's pretty easy when all you eat is bananas! Now for me, I might just decide to eat…a monkey…if you don't stop being obnoxious! Be quiet and pay attention!"

"Ack! You wouldn't eat me!" screamed Loki.

"Nah, you're too scrawny!" agreed Leo. "But be quiet and let the seminar leader do his thing. By the way, what should we call you, sir? You've not yet shown yourself, and I guess you've got a reason for that, but we've got to be able to address you somehow. What's your preference?"

"Thank you for asking, Mr. Lion," replied the Voice. "For now, Leader will do. I promise that you will see me by the end of this meeting."

CHAPTER 2

IT BEGINS

The animals settled themselves comfortably, some in trees and some on the ground, preparing to listen to Leader and learn.

"Throughout time, stories have been used to teach — concepts, values, and history, just to name a few. Today, we'll use a short story, one that happened in this very jungle, to help demonstrate the concepts of decision-making," said Leader.

"In my world, the jungle world you're visiting today, choices are sometimes easier to make than in your so-called civilized one. Here you look for food and water, and avoid danger. While you humans make similar choices and take similar actions, depending upon your personality and values, of course, some decisions have a different risk or danger level."

"Leader," queried Petra, "I'm not certain I understand what you mean by danger level. Could you give me an example?"

"Wait, wait, I know!" exclaimed Loki. At loud groans from the animals around him, Loki continued, "Oh, I know you all think I'm just a silly monkey, but listen. Think about work. If I take the day off, a sick day 'cause I'm sick of work, then there's a danger I'll be found out and get in trouble. Not that I'd ever do that, of course. You know that, right Leo?"

Leo and the other animals laughed, and Leader, with a chuckle, said, "That's a good example of risk, or danger level. The problem occurs when one fails to consider the danger level before taking action. In the jungle, if an animal stops to take a drink from the river but fails to look around for danger, well, the danger of losing one's life is very real. Luckily for humans, loss of life is not usually the danger.

"There are, however, always consequences, and the important thing to understand is that the consequences belong to the individual who has taken the action." Leader continued, "Too often people fail to consider possible consequences and then blame everyone and everything when things don't work out the way they want.

"To our story. Remember, this reenactment deals with making decisions. Let us begin. We will pause at times to discuss the situation and decide how to continue. Consider this an interactive case study, if you will." Leader chuckled and the animals joined in.

"Loki," continued Leader, "in this story I have assigned you the task of carrying an important message to the animals in another part of the jungle…"

"Why do I get the feelin' I'm not gonna enjoy this?" mumbled Loki.

"Oh, quit bein' such a spoilsport," said Petra. "and just have fun with the story!"

"You're not the one bein' picked on," retorted Loki. "It's always me that gets the short end of the stick. How come someone else can't be the one with the so-called assignment?"

"Enough!" roared Lion. "Just do as you're told for once, Monkey!"

"All right, all right, don't get your tail in a knot, Leo. Like, couldn't you see I was just kidding around with Leader? Come on, Leader, start the story and I'll be the best actor you've ever seen!"

"Thank you, Loki, for being so agreeable," responded Leader mildly. "As I was saying, in the story, Loki has been assigned the task of taking an important message to animals in another part of the jungle. The rest of you will be asked to take part in the story as we go along. Everyone ready?" The animals nodded, and Leader continued, "Well then, let's begin…"

The Story:

After being assigned the task of taking an important message to the animals in another part of the jungle, Loki set off bright and early, humming to himself, happy to be given such a simple task. "This job is so easy. I'll just deliver the message and be done in no time. Then I can take a nap," he thought to himself.

"Don't forget, Loki," admonished Leo as Loki walked away, "we're all counting on you…"

"Yeah, yeah, no sweat," replied Loki. "Like I can't handle this! Those animals will have their message in no time."

Walking along the winding jungle path, Loki came upon a river. "Hey, where'd this come from?" he pondered to himself. "I don't recall this river being here before. What am I gonna do?" He wandered up and down the bank, mumbling to himself.

"I'll drown for sure if I try to cross this," Loki lamented. "And if I can't cross the river, no one will get the important message I'm supposed to deliver."

As he paced back and forth, he was startled when his friend, Petra Parrot, suddenly flew up and landed on a rock in front of him. "What's the problem, Loki?"

"What's the problem?! What's the problem?! Can't you see?" Loki cried dramatically.

"What I see is a silly monkey pacing back and forth mumbling to himself," retorted Petra. "I thought you had a message to deliver, so why are you wasting time messing around here by the river?"

"Ack!" cried Loki. "Messing around! What do you mean, messing around? I know I'm wasting time, as you put it! Can't you see? This dumb river is keeping me from completing my assignment!"

"Oh, is that all? All you have to do is flap your wings and fly across, like this." And with that, Petra flew across the river and away, screeching with laughter.

"Dumb bird," Loki mumbled, resuming his pacing. "Everybody knows monkeys can't fly!

"What to do, what to do," he muttered. "There might be crocodiles in the river! Or piranhas! Oh, this is no good, no good at all! If only someone would come along, someone stronger, or smarter, and then I could solve this." He jumped up and down on the path in frustration. "It's just not fair," he screamed, and lay down on the path, sobbing.

The Circle:

As Leader paused in his narration of the story, Loki jumped up and down on his tree branch. "Hey, I wouldn't act like that!" he exclaimed indignantly. "Whoever said I acted like that is way out of line!"

"Oh, I don't know," drawled Leo. "It seems to me like something you would do. I believe I hear the words 'it's not fair' come out of your month about something…pretty much on a daily basis."

"Oh! Oh!" exclaimed Loki. "Now that's pretty low, bringin' up stuff that happens in the office during a seminar. That's not fair!" As the animals laughed, Loki screamed in outrage, swinging from one tree to another.

"All right," said Leader. "Let's all calm down…and that means you, Loki. There are lessons to be learned from this story, and there's something in it for everyone. Remember, keep an open mind."

"You're right, Leader," responded Leo. "I believe I'm learning I need to find a different way to motivate Loki. Each individual is just that, an individual, and has different needs…as well as hot buttons. It's important to remember that."

"Yeah!" exclaimed Loki. "Remember that! I'm different and have different hot buttons. Um, what's a hot button, anyway?"

"I think you've demonstrated very well the concept of hot button, Loki," replied Leader. "A hot button is exemplified by anger or indignation, or some other strong emotion, in response to a comment made by another. In your case, you become angry and hostile whenever you believe you've been criticized or insulted."

"Well," muttered Loki, "Nobody likes being criticized!"

"Indeed they don't," responded Leo. "And I should remember that. I apologize to you, Loki, and promise to do my best in the future to be sure to add a suggestion for improvement whenever I find I have to criticize your work."

Leo continued, "With suggestions, criticism becomes constructive. Without a suggestion for improvement, criticism is simply criticism, leaving the person being criticized feeling angry and resentful, rather than learning for correction purposes."

"Wow!" exclaimed Loki. "I'm impressed, Leo. Thanks. And I'll try to keep from seeing everything as a personal attack, and maybe even ask for a suggestion for improvement if you forget to give me one. That might be kinda hard to do, but I'll try."

"Very good, you two!" exclaimed Leader. "It seems you're making progress! Now, let us return to our previous discussion.

"There are two issues to discuss at this point in the story. As you saw, Loki believes he is unable to complete his assignment because he encountered an obstacle. Obstacles in problem-solving and decision-making can cripple the process, and often times do. Our first point of discussion, then, is to identify the obstacles to solving problems. From your personal experience, someone please give me an example of an obstacle to finding a solution to a problem?"

"I know one," responded Petra, looking at Loki gleefully. "How about lacking an understanding of the problem? It seems to me that in the story Loki doesn't understand the problem."

"Oh, go stick your head in the river!" cried Loki angrily. "You're making fun of me, and I don't like it. I certainly do understand the problem! You're the problem. If you wouldn't have made such a stupid suggestion, I'd have already been able to deliver the dumb message. Fly across, yeah, right!"

"Ha!" snorted Leo. "This is so typical, Loki, blaming everyone else but taking no responsibility yourself. It seems we have discovered two obstacles to problem-solving already. How about it, Leader? Are casting blame and a lack of understanding of the true problem obstacles to solving a problem and making a good decision?"

"They certainly are, Leo," replied Leader. "It seems, though, that both you and Loki have already forgotten your promises to one another."

"Oh, you're right," said Leo. "I'm ashamed of myself. What kind of role model am I that the first opportunity to provide positive reinforcement, I blow it!" Leo hung his head in shame. "I'm sorry, Loki!"

"Ah, forget it, Leo," replied Loki. "I blew it, too. I got mad at Petra and took it personally, when she was just kidding with me. Sorry everybody!" The animals croaked, screeched, and rumbled assurances that it was okay, and to go ahead with the seminar. Everyone, it seemed, was enjoying the show.

"Good, then let's continue." Leader went on, "As Leo pointed out, blame, besides being a complete waste of time and energy, is an obstacle to determining a potentially good decision. And lacking an understanding of the problem certainly doesn't lend itself to a good decision, either."

"Okay, okay, I admit it," answered Loki. "I blamed Petra, or Loki in the story did, and it's not really her fault. And, as far as the problem is concerned, well, that's an easy one. The problem is the river! If not for that stupid river, I could deliver the message in no time and be back in time for my nap…er, I mean, I'd be back in time for my next assignment. Yeah, the river's the problem…dumb river, anyway!"

Leader and the animals laughed at Loki's misstep. "Well, everyone, what do you think of Loki's analysis of the problem? Is the river really the problem?"

"I don't think so," said Leo. "The river is benign, without malice or intent. I think we have another obstacle here. When you allow yourself to become angry, like Loki did in the story," this with a look toward Loki, "it doesn't help solve the problem, and makes it that much harder to find a solution."

"Good," said Leader. "Emotional roadblocks, such as anger, do indeed act as obstacles to finding the true problem, and thus making a good decision."

The group went on to discuss several other obstacles or factors that can inhibit an understanding of the 'true' problem.

CHAPTER 3

THE FIRST STEP...

Following Loki's encounter with the river, Leader and the animals discussed obstacles to determining the true problem — important in the process of making decisions and solving problems.

"Good discussion, everyone!" exclaimed Leader. "We're making progress. Earlier, I said we had two topics to discuss. The first was obstacles to problem-solving. The second involves the steps necessary to making decisions. I believe we can all agree from our prior discussion that our first step to making a good or at least the best possible decision is to..."

Identify the problem — you waste a lot of time and energy when you don't

"Hey, Petra," whispered Loki, "How does Leader talk in italics like that?"

"Silly Monkey," she hissed. "Pay attention and you might learn something!"

"Loki," said Leader, "Are you ready to return to the story now?"

"Yeah, yeah," replied Loki. "If I gotta, I gotta. Just some more making me look like a dumb monkey."

"Hey, if the name fits-s-s-s," replied Snake, evoking laughter from the group.

Loki shook his fist at Sam Snake, making certain he was a good distance away and in no danger of being bitten before doing so, of course.

The Story:

We left Loki at the river, crying and lamenting, with a message to deliver and no closer to his objective. Suddenly he heard a voice.

"Hey, Loki, what's the problem?"

Loki looked around wildly.

"Over here, it's me, Frank…in the river! Why are you carrying on like that?"

Loki spied Frank Fish as he poked his head up from the river. "Oh, Frank, I am so glad to see you! I have to take a message to the other animals. Can you take the message for me?" asked Loki hopefully.

"No," replied Frank, "because I can't walk on land, and it's your mission, anyway. But I'll show you how to cross the river. Watch this." And with that he ducked under the water and came back up on the other side. "See, it's easy! You try it!"

"No, no, no!" screamed Loki in fury, thumping his fists on the path. "Stupid fish! What, are you crazy? I can't hold my breath that long! Go away if you don't have a good idea!"

Startled at Loki's outburst, Frank flicked his tail and swam away.

"Dumb fish!" screamed Loki, jumping up and down on the jungle path. "Why do I have to deal with all these stupid animals? Why doesn't someone fix this problem?"

A deep voice came booming down the path where Loki had begun his adventure. "Loki, stop wasting time blaming others and getting angry," said Leader. "The animals are counting on you! You must determine the true problem before you can expect to discover a viable solution."

"Ack!" screamed Loki. "This is so frustrating. Why won't anyone help me? All I get are lectures and no help!

"All right," Loki said, taking a deep breath. "I know that I'm keeping myself from finding the answer by getting mad and blaming others when they're only trying to help. I know I have to figure out the problem before I can start coming up with answers. The thing is, I don't know what the true problem is! Argh!

"Okay, one step at a time," Loki continued. "I have to take a message to the other animals. That's easy enough and not a problem, except I have this stupid river in my way! This is impossible! I can't do it!"

With that, Loki sat down on the path, put his face in his hands, and sighed despondently.

The Circle:

Loki, hearing the sounds of snickering, looked up to find himself back in the circle surrounded by his animal friends. "Ugh!" he sighed. "Here I am again, needing help and encouragement. Why can't I seem to get this assignment right?"

"Loki, Loki, calm yourself," said Leader. "This seminar is meant to help you discover the best way to make decisions effectively and overcome the obstacles that get in the way to solving problems." He went on, "If you believe something is impossible, it becomes impossible. It is all in your perception of things, the way you see things.

"When you take a negative approach, and look only at the negative, that is what you will likely find. Instead, believe in yourself, have an open mind and follow the guidelines we're discussing today. You can overcome the obstacles and complete your assignment."

"Yeah, Loki," said Petra, "We're all here to learn. You're the one going through all the pain of learning while we try to help. You're doin' great, isn't he, guys?" This to the circle of animals who grunted, squawked, and roared in agreement.

"Yeah, thanks Loki! Hang in there," said Leo, padding over to pat Loki gently on the back in encouragement. Loki, looking surprised at Leo's unusual gesture, patted Leo's paw in thanks.

"All right," said Leader. "Loki is still working on figuring out the problem. Does anyone have any ideas to help him? Perhaps if we talk about a situation in your lives outside our circle here, it might help Loki in his quest. Does anyone have a situation to share?"

"Oh I do!" exclaimed Petra, laughing. "This whole situation has reminded me of something that happened recently. My husband's uncle was due in from out of town for a meeting, and wanted to get together with us for dinner. He would only be in town for the one evening, and there was a conflict. A big one! You see, my car was in the shop, and I had a class to attend that evening. Boy, did we get into it!"

"Why, Petra?" asked Loki. "Wasn't your class more important than eating dinner with your husband's uncle?"

"Well, that certainly was one of my arguments! I had to go to class, it was the night of a big test, and I couldn't make it up." Petra shook her head and laughed ruefully. "My husband and I went round and round! But finally we figured it out.

"You see, like Leader has explained, we needed to find the true problem before we could find a workable solution."

"And what was the problem, Petra?" asked Leader.

"Wait, I think I know," croaked a small voice from the circle. "It wasn't who or what was more important, was it?"

"No, you're right, Freddie, though we did argue about that for a while, along with some accusations from me about him not understanding why getting my degree is important, and accusations from him about me not liking his uncle." Shaking her head, Petra continued, "We wasted a lot of time and energy with that little argument. I wish I'd known then what I've learned here today!"

"Let me tell the problem, please Petra," begged Freddie Frog. At a nod from Petra, he announced grandly, "It was that you didn't have adequate transportation! Isn't that right?"

"Exactly," beamed Petra. "You got it exactly right, Freddie! You must've been there listening!" The animals all laughed, and Petra continued. "Once we figured out that the problem was a lack of transportation, deciding how I was going to get to class while my husband saw his uncle was simple."

"What an excellent example, Petra," said Leader. "I'm sure everyone can think of a similar situation in everyday life. I hope that this has given Loki some insight into his own challenge. From personal experience, I believe the toughest part of decision-making is determining the problem. Once you know the problem, finding a solution becomes simple. What do you say, Loki…are you ready to tackle your assignment again?"

"I guess so," said Loki with a sigh.

The Story:

"Well, here we go again," said Loki. "I'm here looking at the same river, and no closer to getting across and delivering my message."

"Leap, leap," came a voice. "Why don't you leap across?"

"Who said that?"

"Why, I did," answered Freddie Frog. "Leap, leap!" Bunching his powerful legs, the frog leapt across the river and sat looking at Loki from the path on the other side.

"It's too wide," yelled Loki. "I can't jump like you do! I won't make it, and I'll drown."

"Suit yourself," answered Freddie Frog, hopping away.

"Why can't someone give me a decent solution?" Loki agonized, and threw himself face down on the path.

"Why not just walk across?" said Georgia Giraffe. "Look, it's not very deep." But Loki was too busy wailing and whining and didn't hear or see her as she slowly and gracefully waded across the river.

"Well, good-bye then!" called Georgia from across the river as she walked away. "I hope you find your answer soon."

"Argh!" exclaimed Loki. "Why doesn't anyone get it…I can't swim!"

"Ah," said the familiar deep voice of Leader. "That could certainly be a problem."

"No kidding!" exclaimed Loki indignantly. "That *is* the problem!" Sitting up, he slapped the path beside him. "Bring me back to the circle, Leader! I'm so frustrated!"

CHAPTER 4

A BREAK-THROUGH FOR LOKI

The Circle:

"This is so aggravating!" Loki cried. "I can't swim, and you just sit there, wherever you are, and you say, 'that could be a problem'? I'm just speechless! Of *course* it's a problem! Why do you think I'm so upset?"

Loki looked about at his friends and noticed they were smiling and nodding. Scratching his head, comprehension slowly crossed his face.

"Uh oh, I did it, didn't I?" He began laughing, and Leader and the other animals joined in. "Yeah, I did it. You were right, Petra, it was right in front of me all the time. I can't swim. That's the true problem, isn't it? Oh wow! What a relief to finally know the real problem!"

Loki's laughter stopped abruptly, and he hung his head despondently. "But, okay, so now I know, but what do I *do* about it?"

"I'm not certain what you will do about it, since this is *your* assignment," replied Leader. "I do, however, think that now you've identified the real problem, namely that you can't swim, that you can go to the next step in decision-making."

"Yeah, and what's that?" queried Loki moodily.

"The next steps in problem-solving include gathering information and listing possible options for a solution. This is sometimes called brainstorming." Leader continued, "Many of you are familiar with brainstorming sessions from your individual careers. Listing all potential options, without judgment or criticism, is a useful tool in the decision-making process.

"Petra, from your example, what steps did you and your husband take once you discovered that your real problem was a lack of transportation?"

"Well, Leader, what we did was start coming up with ideas about what we could do for transportation," said Petra.

"What ideas did you come up with, Petra?" inquired Loki. "Maybe you could've just flown there, ha, ha! But you didn't have your wings then, did you?"

"Silly monkey," laughed Petra. "No, I wasn't a bird then, just a woman, no wings, sorry! What we did was talk about several ideas, or options, to use your words, Leader. Some of the options weren't very practical, like buying a second car, and renting a helicopter. We really got into it and had fun, which was great since we'd just spent time and energy arguing!"

"I like that," laughed Leo. "Renting a helicopter! Ha!"

"Yeah, like I said, we really came up with some silly ideas, as well as a couple that would work," finished Petra with a smile.

"Excellent!" exclaimed Leader. "This is a great example of brainstorming, everyone. Remember, once you've discovered the true problem, the next steps are…"

"Wait!" interrupted Loki. "Let me talk in italics this time!" Standing stiffly at his full height and thrusting back his shoulders, Loki took a big breath and announced, "The next steps in problem-solving and decision-making are…ta-da…"

Gather information and brainstorm for potential options

The animals and Leader laughed. "Good," said Leader. "So now that you understand the problem — you can't swim — and you seem to have an appreciation for the next steps, then let's send you back to the story and see how you do, shall we?"

"Oh, yeah," said Loki, looking glum. "There is that assignment to finish, isn't there? Oh well, let's get on with it then."

"Now, Loki," scolded Petra. "What happened to your positive attitude and believing in yourself? Come on now, buck up! We're here to help you, remember?"

"Petra is right, Loki," said Leader. "As a matter of fact, I believe one of the animals made a suggestion to you that might help. Why don't you think about it as we return to the story?"

The Story:

"What is Leader talking about?" wondered Loki as he sat by the edge of the river. "Okay, options, options…well, Frank Fish suggested I swim under water, but I can't hold my breath that long, plus I can't even swim, so that one won't work, and to fly, yeah, right! Oh man!

"Wait, when I'm brainstorming I'm not supposed to criticize the ideas, just list them. Yeah, my head feels like there's a real storm goin' on, that's for sure! All right, list the options. Swim across was one, fly over the river was another, leaping like Freddie Frog was another one. What else could I try? H-m-m, I guess I could make a boat or a raft and float across…oh this is just too much!" Petulantly, Loki sat on the path and crossed his arms in front of him.

From the forest came the infinitely patient voice of Leader. "You're forgetting one other, Loki. Georgia Giraffe was here, and gave you a suggestion. You were too busy feeling sorry for yourself, and missed a possible answer to your situation."

"Georgia was here? Oh man, I never even saw her!" exclaimed Loki. "Leader was right! I was so busy feeling sorry for myself, missing the whole point and not knowing that the problem is that I can't swim, that I missed out on Georgia helping me! She could've taken me across the river! Now I'm back at square one!"

"Well, maybe I can help," said a soft voice. Loki looked around and saw Zena Zebra standing near the river where the path ended.

"No offense, Zena, but you can't fly across or leap across, so you're stuck here, like me!"

"You're right, Loki," agreed Zena. "I can't fly or leap, but I *can* swim. And I'll help you cross the river. If you just hold on to my tail, I'll swim across. You'll be safe if you just hang on."

"There's no crocodiles in the river, are there, Zena?" asked Loki nervously.

"No, Loki, there are no crocodiles in the river," said Zena.

"Are you sure there are no crocodiles in the river?"

With a sigh, "I'm sure."

"And no piranha?"

"Loki, there are no piranha and no crocodiles. Now do you want to cross the river or not? I have better things to do than stand here and argue with you!"

"All right, all right, don't get your stripes in a twist! I just don't want to get eaten, you know! But Zena, what makes you so sure it's safe?"

"Because I asked," replied Zena.

"You asked? Who'd you ask?"

"I asked Frank."

"Frank? You mean Frank Fish? How does he know that it's safe?"

Stomping her foot impatiently, Zena replied, "Come on, Loki…he's a fish, he lives in the river, he should know, don't you think?"

"Well, how come he didn't tell me that? I just talked to him a little while ago."

"Maybe it was because you didn't ask him! Now come on!"

With a sigh, Loki clenched his eyes tightly shut and grabbed Zena's tail.

"Could you loosen your grip a bit, Loki?" asked Zena, nipping at him impatiently. "That's my tail, not an old piece of rope!"

"Ouch! You don't have to bite! I'm, sorry! I'm just scared…um, I mean, I'm a bit nervous." At a snort from Zena, he hurriedly continued, "I know…I know…Frank said it was okay. But you know Frank's, he's a little, uh, strange sometimes…I mean he has a funny sense of humor. He might have told you that it was safe thinking you'd agree to carry me across and, and then, when a crocodile attacked, you'd panic…"

"That's enough, Loki," said Zena, interrupting his tirade. "I really believe there's nothing in the river that's going to harm us. Now, would I be swimming across if I thought there were dangerous creatures in the water just waiting for us? Really, you have to trust more and maintain a more positive attitude in life if you ever want to accomplish anything. Now hold on, and keep your head above water."

With that, Zena and Loki crossed the river, with Loki mumbling and grumbling to himself the entire time. Within a few minutes, they were on the other side. As they shook themselves dry, Loki expressed his gratitude for Zena's help.

"Gee Zena, you're really a life saver! If you ever need help with a problem, I'll do the best I can to be there for you!" Gratefully, Loki continued, "Anything at all, Zena, I'm your man. I'll back your play! Really!"

"Well, that's really nice of you to offer, Loki. I'll remember that. Now, don't you have an assignment to finish?"

"What? Oh yeah!" exclaimed Loki slapping his forehead with his hand. "With all the agonizing I did trying to figure out the problem and then a solution, I almost forgot the whole reason for this escapade…my assignment. Well, gotta go, Zena, I've got a message to deliver! See ya!" And with that Loki hurried down the path to deliver his message.

Zena, looking after him, chuckled to herself. "I wonder how he plans to get back across the river."

The Circle:

"Well," said Leader, "it looks as if Loki finished his assignment. Congratulations, Loki!"

"Yeah, well…" replied Loki. "I could've done it a lot sooner if I hadn't acted so badly. But, I did give the animals your message. I don't understand why 'remember to name the elephant' was such an important message, but," shrugging his shoulders, "I did finish the assignment!"

"Yes, you did, and that's really what counts," said Leo. "If I could count on you to complete all your assignments, you and I wouldn't have the, er, issues we do!"

"Yeah, well…um, er, say, Leo, um, do you have any suggestions to help me improve so we don't have our, er, issues?" Loki queried with a grin.

Slapping his head with his paw, Leo retorted, "I guess I deserved that one, didn't I? I should've included a suggestion for improvement with my implied criticism, eh, Loki?"

"Yep, but you'll also notice I didn't get defensive, did I? I guess I've learned something from this seminar after all! What do you say, Leader, am I gettin' better?"

"Yes, Loki, and the true test will be for you to continue to monitor your behavior once you leave this domain," replied Leader. "Now," he continued, "let's discuss the remaining steps to problem-solving and decision-making and see how well Loki followed them in the story. After that, we'll talk about how all this impacts you in your daily life, and then conclude.

"Before we begin, does anyone have any thoughts they'd like to share?"

"Yes, I do, Leader…" began Petra, only to be interrupted by Georgia Giraffe.

"Oh wait, Petra!" cried Georgia. "Before you tell another story, tell us what happened with you, your husband, and your husband's uncle!"

"Oh, that. Well, like I said, once we determined that the real problem was a lack of transportation, the whole thing got sorted out. We started listing all kinds of ideas, which, the way I understand it now, was what people call brainstorming. Anyway, we listed the options. Some were really silly and we rejected them. Others we had to think about."

"What do you mean, Petra?" asked Georgia. "What was there to think about?"

"Well, some of the ideas were ones that could work, but were expensive, or just didn't make sense at the time. Like, for instance, one idea was for me to take a taxi to class and then my husband would pick me up after my class ended. That would work, but I had no idea when I'd be finished with the test I was taking, and he had no idea when he and his uncle would be finished with dinner.

"When we weighed the pros and cons to the idea, we had to drop it since there were too many negatives to make it a workable idea."

"Oh, I understand now," said Georgia. "What did you end up doing?"

"Well, that's really the best part," answered Petra with a laugh. "We finally just called my husband's uncle and asked him what he thought the best plan would be, given we didn't really know what time the meeting would be over.

"Uncle laughed and said he'd pick my husband up at home around seven, and I could meet them at the restaurant after my test. It was such a simple solution! I don't know why we didn't think of it. Well, of course, if my husband and I hadn't gotten into an argument in the first place…but it worked out in the end!" Petra laughed, and the animals and Leader joined her.

"Excellent, Petra!" said Leader. "What a wonderful segue to our follow-up discussion. You provided many excellent examples of the steps you took to making a decision. You were right in stating that you and your husband were brainstorming, so let's talk about those steps, shall we?"

CHAPTER 5

DISCOVERY

Leader thanked Petra for introducing the next step in the process. He continued, "You'll remember we said that the first step in the process is to determine the true problem, and as both Petra and Loki have learned, the true problem is not always easy to find. Once the problem is named, then the process of discovery can begin."

"Discovery?" asked Frank Fish. "You mean like in a lawsuit or something?"

"Well, I suppose it could be compared to that," replied Leader with a laugh. "We're speaking here of gathering pertinent data, information that will help us understand the problem in its entirety. As in Petra's example…"

"Wait, Leader," interrupted Petra. "May I tell?" At Leader's nod, she continued, "Not only did my husband and I not understand the true problem, meaning transportation, we didn't have complete information. We knew his uncle would be in town, and when, but we didn't know whether he had transportation or when his meeting would be completed. Without those pieces to the puzzle, we still couldn't really make a good decision. If we'd known my husband's uncle was planning to rent a car, well, that might have made the entire situation look different."

"Good point, Petra!" said Loki. "And if I had remembered my lack of swimming expertise early on, I would've known the problem and not wasted so much time and energy getting mad and upsetting people who were trying to help me."

"Excellent, both of you," said Leader. "Let's move on. Once you've gathered as much information as is reasonably possible to identify the problem, then it's proper to begin finding options. The term, reasonable, by the way, is very important, as sometimes having too much data is as bad as or worse than not having enough.

"Depending on the type of problem, you may have a lot of data to deal with or a limited amount. Keep in mind the 'who, what, where, when, why, and how' questions when gathering information to name the problem in full."

Leader went on, "Again, once we've determined the true problem, then we begin listing options or ideas, without criticism. This step is also known as brainstorming. Petra, you and your husband did that."

"Yeah, we did, we just didn't realize it at the time." Shaking her head, Petra continued with a smile, "It got to be fun after a while. I can't say we didn't criticize the ideas, though. I'll have to remember that for next time."

"Good idea," replied Leader. "And Loki…"

"Wait, I know I didn't do this step, Leader," said Loki, interrupting as usual. "But I also know that the suggestions my friends tried to give me would have been good examples of the brainstorming step. Like Freddie's idea of leaping across the river or Petra's idea to fly!"

"Correct," said Leader. "I'm quite pleased you recognize this. It's very easy to criticize ideas. The problem with criticism is that it has a tendency to shut down the creative process. People become shy about putting forth ideas if they're being criticized, and since creative thinking is what brainstorming is all about, it's best to avoid judging an idea at all during this part of the process.

"I could spend quite a bit of time talking to you about the creative process," said Leader, "but that'll have to wait for another time. Just remember, the rule in brainstorming is to keep an open mind and refrain from criticism." He continued, "Judging the merits of a particular idea is part of the next step, listing the pros and cons to each idea or option. Begin this step once you've listed all the possibilities you can imagine."

"Oh!" exclaimed Freddie Frog. "Leader, please, might I state the next step?"

"Of course you may, Freddie!" replied Leader.

"Yeah, Freddie, go for it!" exclaimed Loki. "Just belt it out!"

Freddie hopped onto a nearby log, thrust out his chest, and bellowed, "The next step in problem-solving and decision-making is…"

List the pros and cons of each idea or option

"Wow, you are loud!" exclaimed Loki, removing his hands from his ears. "Thanks for telling us that step…I think!" Leader and the other animals laughed, while Freddie proudly took a bow.

"Bet you didn't know I had it in me, didya?" joked Freddie. "Mom always told me I shoulda been on the stage…I can really project!"

"Thank you, Freddie, for your excellent projecting skills!" said Leader. "And you are correct. For each of the ideas you discovered during the brainstorming step, list the pros and cons, the positives and the negatives, the good and bad, still without evaluation."

"Yeah, like when my husband and I decided that my taking a taxi to class could work since the positive aspects meant I could get there on time and take my test. Some of the more negative aspects, though, were the cost of the taxi ride and the length of time it could potentially take for a taxi to pick me up afterward," said Petra.

"Good," responded Leader. "This is exactly what I was talking about. And Loki…"

"Yeah, yeah, I didn't do this step very well, either! I know! I know!" exclaimed Loki indignantly.

Realizing he was getting defensive, Loki stopped, took a breath, and changed his tone of voice. "I'm really glad I came to this seminar now. At the beginning, I thought it would be a waste of time, but I'm really starting to get it! I only hope I'll remember once I get back in the real world and out of this monkey suit." At laughter from Leader and the other animals, Loki said, "What are you laughing about? Oh, yeah," he snickered, "I guess I made a pun, didn't I? Monkey suit. Yeah, right! Ha, ha, ha!"

Loki continued, "Anyway, if I had taken the appropriate steps I might've looked at Petra's suggestion to fly across the river and figured the positives would've been, one, I'd get across quickly, and two, I'd have been the world's first flying monkey."

At snickers from the animals he scowled, then laughed, "Yeah, well, there were those guys that hung around somewhere over the rainbow with that chick and her dog, ha, but to get back to my situation, the downside would've been that I'd have fallen smack in the river if I'd ever jumped out of some tree!

"So, how's that for coming up with the pros and cons for an idea?" Loki asked with a grin, looking rather pleased with himself.

Leader chuckled, "Quite good, actually. I do believe you're getting the hang of it. The other aspect of this step is to project potential positive and negative consequences, so your negative consequence to falling in the river would've been…"

"One very wet Loki!" screeched Petra.

"One very *drowned* Loki," said Leo. "Remember, Loki can't swim."

"Exactly!" exclaimed Loki, drawing a laugh from the others. "Luckily I didn't try, eh Petra? Then I wouldn't be around to pester you anymore!"

"Yes, there's that!" said Petra dryly. "Lucky me!"

"Lucky me!" crowed Loki, giggling.

Laughing, Loki poked Leo in the side and pulled his tail until Leo growled at him, "Stop that, or you won't be giggling long."

Looking affronted, Loki swung up into a nearby tree and sulked.

"Come on, Loki," Zena called up to him. "Get back down here and behave yourself. Silly monkey, don't you know better than to pull a lion's tail? We need you…"

"Yeah, for comic relief," muttered Leo. "Come on, Loki, I won't bite you, I promise."

"Okay," said Loki, brightening, and immediately jumped down from his perch, landing on Leo's back.

"Hey!" Leo exclaimed. "Did I say you could do that?"

"Hey yourself! I thought we were buds again. Don't you love me anymore?" said Loki, scratching Leo behind his ears.

"G-r-r-r! All right, we're buddies! Now, buddy, get off my back!" Leo roared.

"Whoa there big fella, I'm goin', I'm goin'," said Loki. With that, he laughed, patted Leo on his shaggy head, and sprang over to join Petra on her rock. Squawking, she flapped her wings and flew to perch on a tree branch near Georgia.

"All right, everyone, let's get back to business. Loki, behave yourself, please, and Leo, no more roaring for a while. You're making the others nervous," said Leader. Indeed, the other animals were becoming nervous. No one liked it when Leo lost his temper. He was simply ferocious when that happened, and while people thought his bark, or roar in this case, was worse than his bite, no one wanted to test *that* particular theory.

With cajoling from Leader, Leo calmed down, allowing the others to relax.

"Thank you, Leo, for controlling your temper. Loki just can't help himself. He is, after all, a monkey," said Leader, drawing a harrumph and reluctant snort of laughter from Leo. "Well then," Leader continued. "Does anyone have an idea of what the next step in the process might be? Leo, what do you think?"

"Well, I believe the next step, after you've listed the pros and cons for an idea along with potential positive and negative consequences, would have to be to get rid of any option or idea that's obviously not going to work.

"Some of the ideas, like Loki attempting to fly across the river, would likely have many more negative consequences than positive ones. Then, I guess, the rest of the ideas should be put in some kind of order…to find the ones that have the best chance of working out the way the person wants, getting the kind of results he or she desires. How does that sound, Leader?"

"Good, Leo," replied Leader.

"So, as others before me, I shall state the next step!" Rising to his full majestic height, Leo roared, "The next step, or steps, is…"

Evaluate ideas to determine which to discard; rank the remainder in descending order to begin determining which will work best

"Yay!" cried the animals. "Great job!"

"Well, it was easy," responded Leo. "It just made sense to me. However, Leader, before we go on, there's something I want to say. When we talked earlier about understanding the true problem, I meant to emphasize that you've got to understand not only the problem but the scope of the problem as well. I think that is as important as figuring out the problem in the first place. What good does it do only knowing part of the problem?

"You could argue that sometimes a poor decision is better than no decision. But if asking a few more questions to better understand the situation means the difference between a poor decision and a better one, it only makes sense to gather as much information as possible."

Shaking his head, Leo continued, "Decisions aren't always so easy to make. The situations we've been discussing have been some fine examples. On a daily basis, though, problems arise that have far-reaching consequences, some I cannot even begin to foresee. I can't tell you how many times I've ended up with a regular hornet's nest on my hands because I didn't have enough information!"

"That's why," said Leo, "for me anyway, it's better if I have a complete picture. It's frustrating, sometimes, for those who come to me for help, but I've found I make better decisions when I have adequate information."

"What's a hornet's nest, Leo?" asked Loki.

"Well, I've heard people call it a 'can of worms' or a 'Pandora's box,' but for me hornet's nest describes it best. A hornet's nest is when a deceptively simple problem, one you think will be a snap to solve, becomes more troublesome and irritating and harder to solve, the more you look at it." With a rueful grin, Leo went on, "I've usually ended up with a hornet's nest when I didn't ask enough questions or get enough information, and then made a decision based on that incomplete understanding of the problem — and I was usually the one who got stung!"

"Excellent point, Leo," replied Leader, chuckling along with the others. "What I hear you saying is that you like to gather as much data as you possibly can before you consider any of the options. Is that correct?"

"Exactly!" replied Leo emphatically.

"I don't know, Leo," said Georgia. "I think sometimes you can gather too much information. That can cloud the issue, and you can even miss the window of opportunity, as it's called, by taking too long to decide."

"Well, that's true, Georgia. I know I've sometimes had that happen to me," said Leo humbly. "I guess it's like most things in life — you've gotta find balance."

"Balance is a good word," said Petra. "You know, what you're saying even fits in the example I gave about my husband and me. We could've taken so long in discussion, paralyzing ourselves, that we'd have done nothing, except argue and get more and more frustrated with one another. I would've been late for class and my husband's uncle would've had to have dinner by himself!"

"Paralyzing yourself, yeah, kinda like I did with all my whining and moaning," said Loki. "But hey, it worked out all right, so there's no sense crying over somethin' that didn't even happen! So, Leader, what do you think about all this stuff these guys are sayin'?"

"Well, Loki, that's a good question. This has been a very good discussion, and we could spend a great deal of time exploring these ideas. Since we do have a limited amount of time together, let me just say that balance is always a good thing. Keeping that in mind, along with utilizing the steps we're discussing, and adding experience, and patience, we hopefully learn to make wise decisions."

"That's infuriating, Leader," complained Loki. "It sounds like one of those expressions that people say, like, 'you'll know when you know'!" At a laugh from Leader and the other animals, he continued, "And how about 'the more I learn, the less I know'! Doesn't that just blow you away?"

Nodding his head in agreement, Freddie exclaimed, "And how about 'you shouldn't judge a book by its cover', when you know everyone does!"

Freddie continued, "I guess that's the thing about so-called words of wisdom. They're general enough they can be made to fit just about any situation. But you know, they're true, or at least, sometimes…I think." Everyone laughed, and agreed it could get pretty confusing, and that the best thing would be to get back on track and finish the seminar topic they were supposed to deal with before getting into another!

"So, Leader, what is the next step in the process?" asked Leo. "Or should we tell you what we think it is?"

"You seem to be doing well, Leo. Perhaps you can tell me the next step," replied Leader.

"Wait!" exclaimed Petra. "I believe it's my turn!" As everyone laughed, Petra flew down from a tree branch, landed on a large rock and settled her wings. "Well, since we've discovered the true problem, brainstormed for options, eliminated options that won't work, and arranged the remainder in order of viability, to me, the obvious next steps are…" Taking a deep breath, she announced,

Decide, create a plan, and take action

"Very good!" exclaimed Leader. "You are all doing very well. Perhaps I should allow you to conduct the remainder of the seminar!" The animals laughed. "Yes, Petra, that is the next part of the process. And making a decision is really what this whole discussion has been about. This is where it gets interesting."

CHAPTER 6

PEOPLE — THE WILD CARD

"Yes," continued Leader, "at this point in the process, things certainly do get interesting!"

"Why's that, Leader?" asked Georgia. "Wait, I know...you'd think it would be easy to decide now. I mean, we've gone through all the work of figuring out the problem, coming up with ideas, but the decision can still be a gamble. Is that what you mean?"

"Correct," responded Leader. "Depending on the type of problem and its complexity, making the decision still has its risk. No matter how much information you have, or what methods you've used to develop options and consider positive and negative consequences, it is rare that the choice of alternative is clear or automatic. Judgment is almost always necessary, and judgment, as we know, is not always objective."

"Boy, you said a mouthful, Leader," said Leo, shaking his shaggy head. "No matter how scientific the methods I've used to get there, many times when I make a decision I'm thinking, 'What did I miss?' There's almost always something I've not considered, or thought of, and then, of course there's always the wild card — people."

"What do you mean?" asked Petra.

"Ha!" snorted Leo. "People. You just never know what they're going to do! I've come up with some great plans, but, you just never know with people. The ones you think will be the most helpful and cooperative, well, they can just wake up one morning and be totally different. Or at least that's the way it seems sometimes! They're contrary and stubborn! It would be an easy job being a manager if it weren't for people!"

"Oh, I know what you mean," said Georgia, bending her long neck to bring her face in front of Loki. "Just look at this one if you want an example of contrariness! Don't get me wrong, Loki," she began as a look of belligerence crossed his face, causing the other animals to snicker, "you have a lot to offer, but you've got to admit, sometimes you react to situations without thinking, and that can cause problems, some that no one can anticipate."

Butting at him with her head, she continued, "Now stop grimacing, and listen. If you'll think about the story, you'll understand. Do you realize you could've crossed that river any time you wanted? It was shallow enough that even you could've waded across. You were so caught up in yourself, feeling sorry for yourself, and being melodramatic that you missed it. Lucky for you Zena decided to save your sorry self."

"What do you mean?" demanded Loki. "Zena swam across. I can't swim, remember? I think you're being mean, Georgia. You're just mad because I took the wheels off your chair…"

At Georgia's startled expression, Loki continued, "Oops, guess you didn't know I did that, did ya! Ha, ha, you should've seen the look on your face when you sat down. No wonder you're a giraffe here…you're so tall. Whoever set up this seminar certainly typecast you right!" As Georgia leaned in close to Loki, he cried, "Aagh! Get out of my face, ya giant!" Georgia stepped back and laughed.

"See what I mean? Loki, I knew you removed the casters from my chair. And I also knew that if I waited long enough, you'd tell on yourself. See, you made my point, exactly! Thank you, Loki."

"Uh, well, I mean…well, you're welcome, I think," stammered Loki, as he quickly swung up to a tree branch far out of Georgia's reach, mumbling about women being confusing. Georgia and the others laughed.

"Yeah, you got it, Georgia," said Leo. "People can definitely make it or break it for you! And I think considering risk is still an important part of the whole process!"

"True, Leo," replied Georgia. "The thing, I find, though, is to avoid getting caught up in the process to the point where you're incapable of making a decision. Life doesn't stand still, and so, sometimes, despite the lack of an obvious answer, you've just got to go with it!

"Something that helps me when I seem to be stalled at the point of taking action, whether it's risky or not, is to consider, 'What's the worst that can happen, and can I deal with it?' It helps!"

"What do you mean, Georgia? I'm not sure I understand that step," said Leo.

"Wait, wait," cried Loki. "Let me see if I understand what you're talking about! In the example from the story, when Zena offered to let me hold her tail and cross the river, if I'd thought about the worst possible consequence, namely being eaten, and whether I could deal with that possibility…well, I probably wouldn't have crossed the river. So how is that a good thing?"

"Well, Loki," replied Georgia with a chuckle, "perhaps you wouldn't have crossed with Zena in that case, and you'd still be standing at the side of the river. But, the rest of the statement having to do with risk is this: 'If the answer is *yes*, and you can deal with the *worst*, then take the action. If the answer is *no*, the wiser course is to consider other options.' Does that help?"

"Well, I dunno," said Loki. "I think I'm confusing myself here."

"Nothing new about that, Loki," snorted Zena. "Look, still using the story as an example, if you add the fact that I'd already told you it was safe, then your fears should have gone away! Georgia's right," Zena continued. "Sometimes you've just got to go with it!"

"Now wait," said Loki, "I'm really not gettin' this! If I felt the worst possible thing that could happen was to be eaten, and if I don't want to be eaten, why should I have believed you when you said it was safe? I mean, it's my body we're talking about here, isn't it?"

Zena stamped her foot and snorted. "Well," Loki continued, looking startled, "I guess it wasn't just about me, was it. Let me think…okay, I think I may be getting it. Zena made her decision to cross based on information that came from Frank. Information I didn't have. So…if Zena believed Frank, and I believed Zena, and believed *in* her, then my worst possible consequence was invalid. Is that what you're trying to say, Zena?"

"Yes, Loki, that's exactly what I'm saying," cried Zena fervently. "You should have trusted me, trusted in the team! You know I wouldn't intentionally give you bad information, especially if it would impact me in a negative manner as well as you!" Zena went on, "The three of us, Frank, you, and me, have to trust one another to perform effectively as a team! You can be so hardheaded sometimes! Good thing I like you, despite your contrariness!" Loki reached out and patted Zena on the head, then laughed and swung up on a nearby branch when she snapped at him.

"Thank you, Zena, for the great reminder about trust," boomed Leader. "A good discussion, and food for many future sessions. Let's see, though, if we can summarize a bit and stay on track to conclude this session."

The animals laughed, and murmured that it was easy it was to stray from one interesting topic to another, and how it was a good thing Leader was there to help them stay on task.

"I believe we all agree that there is still risk involved in making decisions," continued Leader. "One can never anticipate all possible consequences to an action. All an individual truly controls is what one thinks, feels, says, and does.

"As Leo pointed out, people can, and do, have an impact on even the best of plans. Because control passes from you once you take action, and becomes available for others to absorb and react to, the wild card Leo mentions is indeed an interesting mix in the process. Once you take action, you no longer have control, but you do own the consequences of your action."

Leader went on, "You can see why it is so very important to take the steps we've discussed in making decisions. Once you've determined a course, based on as much information as you can reasonably gather, considered pros and cons, and decided you can live with whatever consequences arise, well, as we said, it's time to create a plan and take action."

"Without looking back, eh, Leader?" asked Leo? "No regrets?"

"Regret is a waste of time, don't you think, Leo?" asked Georgia. "I mean, once an action is taken, and you accept responsibility for the consequences, whatever they might be, then the only reason I can see for looking back is to decide what I learned as a result of the experience."

"Well said, Georgia," responded Leader.

"And I bet I know what comes next," said Georgia.

Learn from your mistakes —evaluate and refine

"Correct," said Leader. "You're all getting very good at this! Once you've taken action, and in some cases endured the consequences of your actions, it's time to reflect. Look at what happened; what went 'wrong,' what went 'right,' and what you might do in the future to improve. I often find it helpful to examine the 'history,' if you will, and find the point where things digressed from the path you intended. That point is where you'll find your opportunity for improvement the next time around."

"Um, er, Leader, um..." began Loki, hesitantly.

"Yes, Loki?" urged Leader.

"Well...that is...I, um, hear all you're sayin' about how important the process is to making a decision. But, um, er..." stalled Loki.

"Come on, spit it out, would you?" growled Leo. "I've never known you to be at a loss for words. Usually you're just goin' on and on without any thought for what anyone else thinks!"

"Well, thanks for the vote of confidence, Leo!" retorted Loki! "I'm trying to do better with that, but you can't even cut me a break!"

"Oh, yeah, you're right," replied Leo meekly. "Guess I've got some room for improvement! But, please, quit beating around the bush and tell Leader what's obviously bothering you about everything we've been discussing!"

"Yes, Loki, please share your concerns with us," said Leader. "Your opinions are just as valuable as everyone else's, and, often that which is left unsaid is the most important aspect to be discussed."

"Well, okay," mumbled Loki. "Here goes. I guess the biggest problem I have with this is the amount of time it has to take to figure everything out. I mean," glaring at the snickering animals around him, "just look at how long it took us to walk through the steps. By the time you're done thinking things through, well, you could've decided what to do, done it, and gone on to the next thing on your list. What good is it to learn this stuff if you miss out on something because you didn't take action in time?"

"Good point!" piped Freddie Frog. "You'd never get anything done if you had to follow all those steps all the time!" A chorus of grunts, chirps, and snorts in agreement came from the circle of animals.

"Enough!" roared Leo. "Do you all have mush in your heads? Think about it! Whenever you learn anything new, it always takes longer to accomplish. As you gain experience, the task becomes simpler. Don't you think it's the same with this? Why would it be any different?"

"Leo's right," squawked Petra. "You've got to give yourself time to learn a new skill! Think about it…when you were learning to walk as a baby, did your parents say to you, 'Oops, you fell. Too bad! No more tries for you! Guess you'll just have to crawl your whole life.' No, they patted you, and told you how wonderful you were, and to try again. And how many tries did you get? As many as you needed, that's how many!"

"It's the same for any skill," Petra continued. "To use some current popular phrasing, give yourself permission to try. Embrace the challenge! As you improve in your use of the decision-making process, you'll find you take the steps almost automatically! As your skills improve, the time necessary to accomplish the steps decreases!"

"Well done, Petra!" exclaimed Leader. The animals agreed, and Petra took a small bow before fluttering up to a nearby tree branch, slightly embarrassed at her outburst.

"Yeah! You go girl!" exclaimed Loki. "Thanks for explainin' that so well! It makes sense to me now. And, you're right, Leader, if I hadn't asked the question, I think it would've distracted me from completely buying in to the process, if that makes sense. I mean, I'm kind of skeptical…" At a burst of laughter from the circle of animals, Loki continued, "No seriously!" More laughter. "Okay, so you already know I'm a skeptic, but that doesn't make me a bad monkey!"

"No, Loki, it doesn't make you a bad anything," replied Leader. "Skepticism is a powerful light under which to place an idea. It's healthy. Just remember to keep an open mind while you're being skeptical."

"Glad to know I'm good for something," said Loki with a grin. "And here you've been complain' about it, Leo." Laughing wickedly, Loki swung over to a branch near Leo, who just shook his head in pretended dismay, and mumbled something about how there would be no living with Loki anymore if he started being right all the time.

Clearing his throat to get everyone's attention, Leader continued, "And, yes, it makes sense that your skepticism could distract you from accepting a new idea, Loki, which in this case is the decision-making process we've been discussing.

"It's always wise to voice your doubts rather than keep them to yourself. It helps to analyze the concept and determine where you need additional information in order for you to accept and embrace," this with a nod to Petra, "that which you're evaluating."

CHAPTER 7

ALL IS REVEALED

Leader asked the circled animals, "Does it make sense to all of you that while evaluating a concept to be sure and ask questions if you need additional information before accepting it?" The animals nodded and grunted their agreement.

"Good, then let's go on. We're coming to the end of the session and need to bring things to closure. We've discussed many concepts today, and learned valuable lessons about ourselves and others, including the importance of trust and patience along with the need for healthy skepticism. We found that in the quest for the perfect decision, we must often settle for the best possible decision, given the constraints of time and circumstance."

Leader continued. "We've discussed the obstacles to effective problem-solving and decision-making, and watched while Loki grew angry and despondent…with himself and everyone in the jungle who tried to help him solve his dilemma. It's easy to laugh at Loki's quandary. Silly monkey, he allowed his frustration to get in the way of the solution and alienated the animals around him in the process.

"In your jungle, failing to name the problem limits your ability to find a viable solution." Leader's powerful voice echoed throughout the jungle, as he continued, "How often are we guilty of such things in our daily lives, throwing away possible solutions to a situation because of anger or some other obstacle?"

Lowering the volume of his voice, Leader said, "Finally, we learned the steps to effectively solve problems and make good decisions, remembering that while not all problems are easily solved, all deserve our time and consideration since we own the consequences of whatever action or inaction we take. So, in closing…"

"Wait!" cried Loki in frustration. "You can't end this yet! Who are you? We've seen bits and pieces of you and know you are wise from your teachings, but know nothing of your face!"

"Have you not yet learned, Loki?" responded Leader. "I had hoped you would realize by now that no one piece is anything but one part of the whole. You must have all the pieces and assemble them before the picture is complete."

Leader sighed, "Ah, but one seminar is not enough to change a lifetime of thinking…you are still Loki. Observe then..." And with that, what had been hidden slowly became visible, no longer obscured by the dense jungle foliage.

"A-h-h!" exclaimed the animals.

"Oh, oh, oh!" exclaimed Loki in awe. "How large you are! You are the mightiest of all creatures!

I bow before you, Master Elephant. You are truly magnificent to behold!"

"Yes, and now that you know how I appear in whole, you understand the mystery of the many pieces you've seen before," said Elephant. "Tell me," he continued, "what you have learned from this statement."

"Oh, I get it!" exclaimed Petra. "In decision-making, which is what this seminar is about, it's important to understand the whole, the big picture, by assembling all the pieces…before you can make a good decision."

"Very good, Ms. Parrot! You have discerned the answer. Do any of you remember the story of the blind men and the elephant?"

At the looks of puzzlement from the circled animals, Elephant continued, "It is an old Hindu story, in which each of six blind men touched a part of the elephant and thought the part he touched was the whole. One grasped the tail and thought the elephant was like a rope, while one touched the ear and thought the elephant was like a fan. Another grasped the tusk and thought the elephant was like a spear, and so on.

"We know that the elephant is not any one of those things…"

"Yeah, you don't look like any old piece of rope to me!" exclaimed Loki.

"Why thank you, Loki," responded Elephant. "However, as much as I appreciate the compliment, I'd appreciate it more if you'd allow me to finish my lecture."

"Ah, yeah, sorry," said Loki, hanging his head.

"It is your nature, Loki," said Elephant, "to interrupt and behave foolishly, though you do have the power to change your behavior. Such is the strength of humans. You choose your thoughts and actions, and once you've chosen, you — and only you — own the consequences of those actions.

"It is the opposite sides of the same coin. One side is freedom, of choice and action, while the other is the constraining factor of responsibility for the consequences of your actions. It is important you understand this duality. It is a fundamental aspect of life, this freedom and constraint.

"But I digress. To return to our original discussion regarding the blind men and the elephant, the blind men could not discern the whole, or the elephant in this instance, so could not make a proper judgment regarding the aspect of the elephant.

"So, too, is the case in the effort to make good decisions," Elephant continued. "Until you understand the whole picture, or as much of it as is possible in any given situation, you will be as the blind men, vainly trying to describe the elephant based on incomplete information...in the process making a potentially incomplete, or even wrong or disastrous decision.

"Use the steps we've discussed today to help you in solving problems and making decisions," Elephant said. "Begin by seeing the 'elephant' or the whole or true problem — you cannot ever hope to make a good decision without having the whole picture. Get in the habit of asking yourself, 'What does this elephant look like?' You have to name the elephant, describe it accurately, before you can ever hope to resolve an issue, solve a problem, or make an educated decision."

Nodding his head fondly at the circled animals, Elephant went on, "Then, by following the steps we discussed, break the 'elephant' into smaller 'bites' or pieces. Remember, an elephant is overwhelming in size and must be reduced to smaller parts to keep you from giving up before even beginning.

"What you have learned — what you've gained today — is an opportunity, an opportunity to go forward with knowledge. What you do with that opportunity, with that knowledge, is up to you. It's your decision."

With that, the jungle scene disappeared, and the seminar participants found themselves sitting around a large table in the middle of a very nice, albeit very ordinary, hotel conference room. Looking around in a bemused manner, they smiled at one another, collected their belongings, and began leaving the room.

"Wasn't that something special?" breathed Petra to Lon. "I mean, how often do you get the opportunity to experience something so fantastic? I can't wait to get back to the office and talk to the others about it! Maybe they'll get the chance to go through what we did sometime soon!"

"What experience?" asked Lon petulantly. "Just another dumb seminar if you ask me."

"What are you saying?" squawked Petra in astonishment. "Are you going to tell me you don't think that was the most exciting seminar you've ever experienced? After all the things Leader taught us, showed us, helped us learn! You can't possibly mean it when you say it was just another dumb seminar!"

"Don't get your feathers in a tizzy, Petra," replied Lon, laughing. "Remember, skepticism is good for you!" With that, he plucked a red feather from Petra's shoulder, waved it in her face, and walked away, whistling merrily.

LEADER'S STEPS TO SOLVING PROBLEMS AND MAKING DECISIONS

- Identify the problem — you waste a lot of time and energy when you don't.
- Gather information and brainstorm for potential options.
- List the possible positive and negative consequences of each potential solution.
- Evaluate ideas to determine those that need discarding; rank the rest in descending order to determine which will work best.
- Make a decision, create an action plan, and take action/implement the plan.
- Learn from your mistakes — evaluate and refine.

ABOUT THE AUTHOR

Barbara J. McAdoo is a veteran in the world of presentation and public speaking. She's been an instructor, presenter, consultant, technical writer, manager, leader (and there *is* a difference), career counselor, and — most importantly to her — a good student.

A desire to help people grow personally and professionally has kept Barbara inspired through the years — along with a fascination with people and the way they behave — and she is a passionate advocate of lifelong learning. To paraphrase the words of one of her favorite speakers, *you're either green and growing or ripe and rotting.*

The best way to teach is to share, Barbara believes, and she has done so successfully in both the private and public sectors for over 20 years. Combining wit and wisdom with compassion and conviction, along with laughter — and sometimes tears — she has delivered her message to over 20,000 individuals in the U.S., Canada, and Great Britain.

Barbara has been a contributing writer in the *Journal of Educational Media & Library Sciences;* has authored two components of *353 Adult Education Project: Teacher Handbook for the Functional Skills Project With Applied Performance Assessments;* has published hundreds of articles in professional periodicals, and is the creator of *many* original seminar modules. This book, *Naming the Elephant,* is the first of several Barbara plans to extend her message: every human being has the power to be happy and personally fulfilled.